I0426825

Now I'm Riding
My Tadpole
ISBN 978-1-365-25985-2

ISBN 978-1-365-25989-0
Now I'm Riding
My Tadpole

in memory of
Clifford Booth
1932 - 2008

Table of Contents

chapter 0

Preface

For years I rode a Cannondale, an all aluminum, standard two-wheeled upright bike. Then a few years ago I had a brain stem stroke and after quite a bit of therapy, I recovered nicely. There was still a problem though; I couldn't ride my bike.

Well, that's not exactly true. I could ride, but only in a straight line. If I had to turn, left or right, I chanced falling down. Not only could I fall into car traffic, but I could also injure my riding buddies. A doctor told me that I was lucky that this was all I was worried about, he said it was pretty common for a stroke to cause a person to lose some of their balance.

I complained to everyone I saw. A few days later, on my desk was a catalog of three wheelers from Terra Trike. It turns out, several of my bike riding friends frequent the same hobby shop as I do (Flightline Hobby in Lake Orion, MI). One of my friends heard my complaint and sent the catalog with Joe, my office-mate. I looked at the catalog for months, and then finally decided which model to buy and calculated how long it would take me to save enough money to buy one. My wife urged me to to check out other brands. Terra Trike had an advantage being based in Michigan, but other brands like Catrike, KMX, RANS, Maxarya, Sun, Optima, Easy Racer, and others would all be considered. All make three wheeled recumbent tadpole units that will be on my list.

So what's a recumbent tadpole?

Any *"recumbent"* has a seat that reclines and your feet are usually on pedals out in front of you. A *"Tadpole"* is a kind of tricycle, with two wheels in the front of the rider that steer and break and a single one behind the rider that pushes the rider forward. The other kind of tricycle is called a *"delta"* and has one wheel in the front and two in the back, behind the rider, like a child's big-wheel. Depending on the model, one or more of the rear wheels are driven by the pilot. There even models that are front wheel drive!

Three-wheels The three wheels solve most of my problems. I don't have to worry about my balance failing me at just the wrong time and making me take out one my friends. My trike is super stable, with three wheels on the ground most all the time.

I'm riding again now! It reminds me of days of old. The wind flowing through my hair, what there is left of it. Being out so far that the only thing I can hear are my own tires on the pavement. I should have bought a trike years ago.

My Cannondale two-wheeler, I still have it, but it needs

a new set of tires. Eventually I'll give it away to someone who will use and appreciate it. Me? I'll never go back.

The trike is the way to go for me. A comfortable seat. The ability to stop peddling without putting your feet down. Your arms don't carry any of your weight.

chapter

1

Find your dealer

For years I didn't seem to have much need for a dealer - scratch that, I didn't but my father did. He had a friend in a bike shop owner in the next town over. Each of the bikes he bought as gifts for me came from that shop, including the Cannondale that I have now. My father was (he has passed since) a retired master mechanic. I didn't need a dealer's mechanic very often, we even had a set of wrenches ground down so they weren't very thick. Now that he has left us and I'm older, a dealer is very useful indeed.

In addition to your trike or bike, you will need some other stuff -

you'll need	helmet
	shoes
	peddles
	water bottles
	a flag
	a set of tires (now and then)
	clothes
	bike computer
	tools

If you read the preface, you know that I'm in the market for a trike. I mentioned this to my friend, Bud. He called me and said that his friend (an expert on trikes) told us to check the local dealer because rumor has it that they have some trikes in stock. I called the dealer (yep, they had every kind of trike in stock). I called Bud, and told him the good news. Bud said he'd pick me up for lunch, then head over to Al's, the bike dealer.

This is good for me because I get to barrow some of Bud's good luck. Let me level with you, I have bad luck. In fact, if it wasn't for bad luck, I'd have no luck at all. This is how bad it is. My wife, Jenny and I had just spent three or four days in Los Vegas and we were at the airport waiting to board our jet home. It's my habit to have some chewing gum before the flight. I put a dollar in the change machine, four quarters fell into the tray and I remember saying loudly "jackpot". The best I had done all week!

The showroom is rather large and most of the trikes are in the first row, closest to the door. These were all beautiful machines, but not what I was looking for. I saw one tech by the counter near the rear of the showroom, I said
"do you have any tadpoles"
"there's one right there", he said, pointing down the third isle.

It was gorgeous. I met the tech at the trike.

"Can I sit on it?", I said.

"Sure" he replied.

I sat down, my first recumbent seating – it's just like sitting on a beach chair. The seat was comfortable. Nothing like the saddle on my two wheeler.

My friend asked "can he take it for a ride around the parking lot?

"Sure", replied the tech, which we now know as Steve.

He lifted the trike over his head and carried it to the front door. The tech sat the recumbent down. I sat down on it, I started out pointed north on the fairly large parking lot. I rode to the north western edge of the parking. I made a left hand "U" turn and rode over to Bud. I told him "I like it."

In reality, I had to have it. The trike was just what I needed to ride again. In less than a week, I owned that very Sun recumbent! I should say that this trike is the first of it's kind from Sun. It's the ECO TAD SX. The cycle is pretty inexpensive ($950, the cost of a well made trike or bike). Soon I had paid for the trike and arranged to have my friend Bud bring his full size Chevy truck to carry the trike back to my house.

Your dealer will know exactly what fits your bike or trike, and they may even have a good guess what fits you and what you might like. You may think that you'll save a bunch of money buying from the INTERNET, instead of your dealer. Not so. You will find that you only save a bit of money buying on-line if any at all!

My helmet story...

Several years ago I went to downtown Flint, Michigan to

see a bike race of about thirty category three racers. There was a regular amateur rider near the start/finish line, he wanted to cross the street. He waited for the riders to pass then crossed the road on his bike. When he reached the curbing on the east side of Saginaw Street he tried to jump his Schwinn up onto the sidewalk. He didn't make it, he fell and hit his head on the cobbles, he was knocked out. An ambulance was called, the racers steered around it for the several laps that it was there. The attendants put the rider in their vehicle for a trip to the hospital. His undamaged bike was stood up on the sidewalk.

Ever since that day I have always worn a helmet on every ride. I don't mind looking a little funny as long as I don't have to take an unplanned ride in an ambulance.

Buy a helmet of bright colors and CPSC and / or Snell B-95 certifications. My current one is red, before this one, I had a white helmet. Any color that will be seen by a car driver is good.

Why you might need new shoes and peddles...

When you buy a new trike, you'll get peddles with it. But they may not do the entire job for you. When you get moving pretty good, one of your feet may fall to the ground. Your foot will find a way to attach itself to the road or path you are on and your trike will continue on until your foot is trapped under and behind your front wheels. It will hurt – I'm speaking from experience here.

For a handful of years, I've used the same pair of "clippless" shoes and peddles. I have to admit they have worked well. I was so sure that they would keep working, that I had the dealer install the peddles from my Cannondale on my new Sun trike. They worked ok for a while but the material that the heels were made of had broken down and no longer held my feet correctly.

You will have to have pedals that accept the cleats that your shoes have. If your pedals accept SPD cleats then you need SPD shoes. Usually, pedals come with a set of cleats. Your dealer will put these on for you.

I now have a pair of SerFas brand road shoes that I bought from my dealer. I screwed on my existing cleats (SPD-SL style - three screws) Don't forget that if you buy your shoes from your dealer you can try them on before you buy them. A major plus. If you buy shoes through the net and they fit, "congratulations!" and don't forget, you've used up some of your good luck.

Water bottles

I use water bottles. Even when my friends were using Camel Bck hydration systems (CamelBak is a brand name) or other fancy hydration systems I still used plain old water bottles. I often know how many bottles of water a section of road may take. My new trike will accept four braze-on water bottle cages (two, one on each handlebar and two more on the back of the seat). I can't imagine a ride that requires more than four bottles of water without a stop. Four ought to be plenty. I only had two on my Cannondale and that worked for me for a bunch of years.

I have accumulated several of the thermos style bottles (Polar and Schwinn brand) and several others including one from Al's, my local dealer where I bought my trike. Sometimes you'll get one free from a shop if you buy some significant gadget, or ride a fairly long ride, you might get a bottle bearing the sponsor's name and phone number.

A flag.

If you're going to ride a trike, you should have a flag. A trike is low to the ground and there are points in the road where you are lower than some traffic. The flag will fly three or four feet above your head letting the on-coming driver know that you're there. Flags are usually made in two pieces with a joining tube in the middle. I put a couple of drops of glue in that section. That should keep those two sections together. You should still have a brightly colored helmet. Now, I have a flashing light on my left handlebar. If I know that I'm going to be in some heavy traffic, I will turn that thing on. It's just one extra gizmo that will bring a driver's attention to me.

a set of tires (now and then)

Well, it's coming to the end of the summer and I've noticed significant wear on my tires. There is no tread to speak of, although the trike still turns and breaks well. I mentioned that I bought a new pair of shoes, well I told the tech that I wanted some new 100psi tires for my trike (I'll be riding some long rides on the trike next year). The tech said he'd put the new set of tires on while I waited.

I asked about the factory tires. The tech said that they will go about two hundred miles of the type of riding that I do. The new tires are also Kenda brand, but they have a much longer useful life. I might not be surprised if I can make this set of tires go more than 500 miles. The fact is that the 100psi tires make the trike feel more like the Cannondale. What's cool about these tires is that they cost less than $30 each and they put them on for $18 for all three, while I waited! The higher pressure tires have a smaller tire patch on the ground. I've noticed that more even breaking is called for. As the rider applies the brakes the tire patch increases and the rider has less trouble with the rear wheel swinging around to the left or right. This is unlikely to ever occur with the factory tires.

Other high pressure tires are Big Apple brand and Schwalbe brand. If you're going to put a lot of miles on your trike, you will be putting some brand of high pressure tires on your machine.

The tech told me that the two front tires will wear a bit faster than the center rear tire since those tires do all the turning and braking Don't forget that the front tires are off the center of the torque that you produce.

clothes

It doesn't matter much what cloths you wear. In the case of my upright bike I wore apparel that was designed just for an upright bike. Shorts were made with padding in them. Jerseys are about the same. Gloves usually had some extra padding in the palms.

With the trike, you can wear just about anything that you're comfortable in. There are shorts that have adjustable cuffs, and jerseys usually are adjusted by a built-in zipper.

Bike computer

I should say that there are dozens of good bike computers available, you might want to do a bit of research before you buy one. Several have GPS features (they receive GPS positional data from US military satellites in orbit around the earth). I've been "a simple is better" kind of guy for a long time now, so I left my Planet Bike unit on the Cannondale road bike and ordered a new Cateye Velo 7 unit for my trike. The Velo 7 are inexpensive and easy to set up, they don't include any GPS capabilities. I don't like wireless things, so I like the wired Velo. The wired unit always works, so once it's hooked up (I'll tell you how) you'll have no problems. The battery lasts more than a year!

How all these units work is this: for every rotation of each wheel, the bike/trike travels the distance of the circumference of the wheel. So for my trike, every time the wheel makes one trip around, the trike goes the distance of the outside of one of the 20 inch tires. The part in motion is a magnet. The sensor is a reed switch that closes for part of a second, every time it is in the field of the magnet. The computer has to count the rotations of the wheel and compare the distance traveled over the time it has measured. In our case, the magnet is hooked to the most inner part of a leg of the right break disk. I used a plastic zip tie to affix the magnet to the break disk on the right wheel of the trike – if you use the brake a great deal (you frequently ride a trike down a mountainside) you may find that this location will be too hot and the zip tie might melt off.

The magnet is held on by a zip tie and a drop of glue on the break disk. The reed switch (hanging below the axle in this photo) is placed in the plastic holder zip tied to the axle.

Tools

You need at least a few tools to take care of your bike. Don't forget the air pump, I would suggest consider a decent floor model – I use a Joe Blow model made by Topeak. You will need a hex wrench to put on your water bottle cages. You have to have a regular straight blade screw driver. You might as well get a fair number of Phillips screw drivers too. As for wrenches, thinner units are required for bikes than for cars. Bike wrenches are often stamped out of 3mm steel, your car wants you to use wider cast steel units. Most bikes require metric wrenches. Some fasteners on your bike may be American sized. You probably need a chain cleaner device, mine is made by Filzer.

Don't forget - your dealer will have all the tools needed to keep your bike or trike in perfect working order with the knowledge how to get the right results. I highly recommend that you take advantage of this fact.

chapter

Emergency on road kit

Every person I know has had a flat tire at least once in a while. I often wonder if it is impossible to avoid this fate and I'm just not sure that it is. You should be ready, no matter what, to have this sort annoying thing happen to you. You need a few items, you can get from your dealer or Amazon or a dozen other places on the web.

Things you must carry in the US
tube (for the size of your wheels)
pump (to fill the tube to the desired pressure)
tire patch (to stop up holes in tubes)
a $20 dollar bill
tires levers(you'll need at least two)
cell phone(my case holds my FG 510E &
my LG800 smart phone)

My Cannondale has skinny tires and a couple of times I had to replace one bad tube and then applied a patch to a second tube. So I know that it's against the odds but it does happen to have two flats on the same ride.

My new trike has to have a different emergency kit. Yours should too. You probably have to have a Schrader valve pump. Schrader is the same type of air valve that your car has, your road bike probably uses Presta valves.

The other thing you must remember is that the front two tires (on a tadpole trike) must be accessed from the outside of the unit. The rear tire is accessed the same way as on a two-wheel bike: the repairman (you) will unhook the rear wheel with the quick release. You'll use your tire levers to unseat and remove the tire. Then remove the tube, but check the tire for any foreign material that may have caused the tube's failure. If your tire is damaged put your $20 dollar bill in the damaged area to protect your tube as you ride back home or to your dealer for a more permanent repair). I always carry a $20 with my trike, in case I need a ride home. A $20 bill might cut it for a trip back home or to the dealer. You'll need at least one new tube for your kit! I always start every long ride with new or unrepaired tubes.

There is a time that you can wait for a SAG wagon or van (provided on most organized rides - support and gear) vehicle in case you don't have all the gear you need . Often a ride in a SAG wagon is for people who are unprepared and a ride in one will come with a bit of trash talk from other riders in your group.

This is my kit for my two wheeled bike my trike would use the same kit with a 20 in. tube and a pump set for the Schrader valve.

You might want to use a carbon dioxide tire inflater instead of a pump. A CO2 inflater is simple, easy, fast, and light in weight. The major pro to the CO2 inflater is it's fast and fills your tube in a fraction of the time it takes to do the same with your mini pump. The cons are a few. Since a whole cartridge is used to fill most tires, you can't loan this to another rider unless you have an extra cartridge with you. If I remember my college chemistry very well, the CO2 molecule is both smaller and pointed in such a way that your tube will deflate faster than if it was filled with breathable air (about 80% nitrogen).

My CO2 tire inflater – it uses 20 gram CO2 cartridges

To fill up your tube, screw the cartridge into the silver part of the Genuine Innovations airchuck.

Push On and Up increases inflation, pulling the chuck back allows gas to seep out. I bought 10 twenty gram cartridges in case I really got to like this thing. That didn't happen yet, so I'm still using the Joe-Blow by Topeak floor pump.

One thing that I really like about the floor pumps is that most of them have a built-in pressure gauge. The Joe-Blow model has a rota-able plastic ring around the gauge with an arrow that you point to your desired pressure. For me the desired pressure of about 95psi on all three wheels for my trike.

chapter 3

Security

Depending on where you must store your bike you will change the way you secure your bike. I live in a housing complex and my trike lives in the front room. My wife, Jenny says that it should live there, just to be safe. My Cannondale lives at my office, not far from my desk. The fact that they are both indoors keeps them safer than an average bike.

To put them outside you will need a few things. First, you will need a lock. I chose a couple of small units meant for a motorcycles and other expensive stuff. The first of these comes with three keys. One of the keys is a little larger than the other two and has an LED embedded into it to provide a bit of light, should you need to unlock your unit when it is dark out. Both are made by Masterlock. One lock is called a Trimax Max60 and the other is called a Masterlock No. 40. The Trimax Max 60 requires an oiling right away for it to work for me.  I grabbed my WD-40 can, then I just spayed a tiny bit of oil into the holes where shackle goes and a bit in the key hole. This one uses a type 2 key which makes the lock harder to pick, The other round lock is generally well known. The bad thing about this is that there are several youtube videos on the INTERNET about how to pick the type 40 lock. The good news is that the lock is stainless steel so it still works well outdoors.

Next, I bought a braided cable also from Masterlock. A long, 15 foot cable, which should allow me to lock my bike or trike to any fixed item, a fence post, a wall stud, a ground pipe or even the bike rack. My friend Cory said that he could attack the cable with a die grinder and a cut-off wheel. He's probably right. He'd be through it in a couple of minutes. You should hope that there are many easier to take and fence bikes present. This is one time when the length of the trike may come in handy.

I like brass locks. They come in many different designs, some allow you to choose your own combination, but best of all, they work in any weather. There is sometimes a downside to these, they often have a brass shackle that is easily broken or sawed. But wait, you can buy brass locks with a steel shackle. That means that you have the weatherproofing of the brass lock with the security of the steel shackle.

Chains are said to be less vulnerable to attack than cables, especially those chains with trapezoidal or square links (all four sides are hardened). I've also been asked who wants to use a chain that weighs more than the bike it is protecting.

On your upright bike usually three of the tubes, the seat tube, the down tube, and the top tube, form a triangle. As long as your lock, chain or cable passes through this triangle you will be able to fasten your bike to an immovable object like a sign or parking meter. In the case of a trike you've got a different problem – no triangle – there is no way to tie your frame to your immovable object. WAIT I have an idea, What if I place one of those big loop bike locks right were the front axle bar crosses the center frame member. I'll try it. It WORKS

The loop lock is made of 3/8th inch hardened steel – almost uncut-able. You can see in the picture that I have passed the big bike lock through a loop of the cable. You must lube this lock, the keyhole and both shackle holes deserve a couple of drops of WD-40 so you don't have to pay your dealer to cut it off for you. I had to ask for their help.

I once heard a story about a tadpole being stolen near my house. It seems a little odd from the standpoint that no pawn broker would want a tad. Tadpoles are just too long and take up too much floor space nor will they hang on a standard bike hanger. On the other hand it never hurts to set up an account with the NationalBikeRegistry.Com. It only costs $10 for the next ten years. I did it.

There's some bad news. It really doesn't matter how much you spend or how well you do your homework, for $20 you can buy a bolt cutter that will defeat almost anything that you are likely to buy no matter how you use it.

I found a website where the owner says that making your bike ugly will stop bad guys from taking it. Painting it all matte black or all white is a good start. Maybe a good choice is to put a hole in the saddle and some fake animal fur can't hurt. The more you do and the uglier your bike is the less likely your bike or trike will be stolen.

chapter 4

Can you tip your trike over?

Yep, you can tip the trike over - but it's not easy and you are usually surprised when it happens. It happened to me.

I'd been having some trouble with my shoes. I had ridden my

trike to church that day. My planned route was eleven miles there. About nine miles on my way back, I started to have a problem where my left foot started to come out of the left shoe. The shoe stayed clipped to the peddle but the foot came right out! I unclipped the shoe from the peddle then placed it on the ground and put my foot back in it. For some strange reason each time I did this, I had significant trouble clipping the left shoe back to the peddle, slowing my trip home. This happened several times – I have to face it, the shoes are old and have to be replaced. I noticed that all the new shoes have at least three straps to hold your feet in. My old shoes have only two Velcro straps. The old ones worked fine for a bunch of years with my upright bike. But they don't work so well with the new trike. Make a mental note, stop at the dealer and get some new shoes.

I took a minor detour and fixed my shoe again. I got back on my original route. I had to stop again, my foot popped out of the shoe. I had just passed Williams Gun Site company on Lapeer road. I put the right foot in the shoe with no trouble. I unclipped my left shoe by hand and put the shoe on the ground. In less than a second I had fallen to the right. My right foot was still clipped in the peddle so the trike was on top of me. It only weighs about 45 pounds so it was no big deal to move. I unclipped my right shoe and pushed the trike back up to the road shoulder. I must admit that I was a little confused by the entire experience, probably because I had never fallen in over a hundred miles. Several folks were climbing into their vehicles in the parking lot at Williams and saw me disappear into the ditch and came to my aid. First there were a couple of fairly strong men who insisted on helping me up the steep ditch grade. Then there was a generous man and woman who offered to put my trike into the back of their pick-up truck and take me home (only about two miles away). I accepted their offer and they put my trike in the back of their truck, in minutes, with their help, I was home.

I made a trip to the dealer for a new pair of shoes. The problem is solved now. I have new shoes and I know what to avoid. Be careful if you're used to upright bikes, trikes must follow the terrain. When the ground is steep, your path will be steep.

chapter 5

Shakedown ride?

In years gone by I used to write notes of rides that I took, often I would read them and play the whole ride back in my memory. I certainly don't expect you to do that. But, when you get a new machine you have to take it for a shake down ride. You should pick a place that easy to call from and where you can have a few tools with you. For my two wheeler/ I chose a shopping mall right in the middle of town.

I'm sure that I wrote a few notes after my shake down ride of my Cannondale two-wheeler. The original notes are missing or have been destroyed.

Cannondale.

I remember that I needed a new set of tires. The tires that it came from the factory with were good Continental brand but I learned right away that aluminum fames are less giving than steel, If I ran over a dime I could tell you if it was head or tale. I replaced them with IRC Triathlon triers. A much better ride. I needed a set of handle bars that were a bit more narrow – provided by Scott Cycling Products The saddle that the bike came with too much foam, I think I ordered a new saddle by Bella. It fit well and worked good. Within a couple of weeks, a couple of wheel repacks and some T-9 Boeshied chain lube and a new set of tires now & then. I've ridden this Cannondale two wheeler thousands of miles.

Sun-Eco-Tad-SX

I rode the Sun trike around the apartment complex near where I live. Luckily, my friend Bud had his truck at my place and chatted with my wife for the short while that a shake down ride would take. I was impressed with the build and set up quality of the trike. I moved the seat forward about a half inch. That was it there were no real problems with the Sun trike. It only took me about twice on my short route to realize that I was waay out of shape and would not be able to ride my favorite mass-start rides. A new season is going to start and I already feel better than last year.

chapter 6

Rides!

When you got your first bike, the bike becomes a vehicle of freedom. It takes you places. It lets you go places you would not be able to go otherwise. Your new bike may make you feel the same way.

I started to ride for the cardio exercise reasons. Compared to running, biking is easy on your knees, keeps you cool while you exercise, and let's you see things that you haven't seen before. One Saturday morning I was riding quietly on a street near my home and saw a fox. Super rare to see such a beautiful wild animal on a public street.

Another thing that happened that is my own fault. The phone has become my master. We got a fancy phone system made by Ericson. It allowed any company or person to leave as many messages as they would like to. That's not all. I gave every customer a special service number then I bought a pager (remember those?) it called and told me the customer's service number. I would call the customer and remind them that I don't know their passwords.

This is your short warm up ride.

Don't take your pager. If your cell phone is used for work. Don't answer any work call.

You should have a short ride that you can cover in less than an hour. You can ride this route when you get home. My current warm up ride is seven miles in length. I have had an eleven mile warm up ride for several years. But my new ride has a couple of hills, about thirty five feet high. I've decided that the hills are more valuable than the extra distance.

My short warm up ride begins on the North entrance of the Charter Oaks Apartment complex. By turning West I am confronted by a hill in Lapeer Rd. I climb this hill and coast down the hill then turn North along Irish road. The paved bike/pedestrian path offers passages past the I-69 entrances and exits. I continue North and then turn right and then ride east on the path until I almost reaching Gale Rd. I make a "U" turn in less space than my upright bike takes. Once I reverse my path, I ride to the driveway that exits the Meijers parking lot to the South. I ride onto Lapeer Rd. which is four lanes wide. I climb up the hill then coast down the East bound side. I usually ride trough the apartment complex on my way home.

Saturday ride

My Saturday ride is about 30 miles long, I call it a Saturday ride because most Saturdays start with this ride. The first leg of my ride is North on Irish to Richfield Rd. Now onto Northbound Vasser Rd. I ride North on Vasser to Carpenter Rd. East on Carpenter Rd. till you reach Belsay Rd. Follow Belsay Rd. North. until it ends really it turns left and becomes Stanley Rd. Ride till you reach Genesee Rd. Across the road (Genesee) there is a sidewalk that connects to the paved walk/bike path. The first section of the path is through old woods and the path winds gently through them. During the second two weeks of May you will see more trillium flowers in bloom than any other place you're likely to go. I finish the first section and determine if I need more water. If I need more, I can fill empty bottles at the manual pump. The pump is near the boat ramp, you can't miss it.

I ride the second section of the bike path to the West of the parking lot. I always dismount, sit & rest while I watch the lake waves from a western facing bluff.

When I'm ready to move on, I hop back on the bike then ride south and take the path that crosses the road and continues on down the third section of the bike path. This section replaces the damaged piece of Carpenter road.

Before I go on to explain the remaining bike path, I'll tell you about the closure of Carpenter Rd. At the corner of Center Rd. and Carpenter Rd.. you will see some large road closure signs at the top of the hill. The road was closed because the lake had undercut the soil that supports the roadway. Part of the road has fallen away.

The third section is a path that wonders through the woods and goes from Center road to Stanley road – the road that takes us to Steppingstone Falls.

Now for the forth section of the path. If you ride up the hill on the winding path you will emerge at BlueBell Beach. If you follow the path you will find yourself on the concrete walkway by the beach. Ride slowly and carefully since there may be swimmers or children on the walkway. If you stay on the walkway you can ride up past the men's and women's washrooms, past where the PennyWhistle Place used to be. Now we'll ride across the parking-lot (it's usually empty) to the exit side of the driveway, Exit to the North on Bray Rd. I ride North on Bray Rd to Mt Morris Rd. - just another mile and a half or so. I turn right on Mt. Morris and ride all the way to Irish Rd.. Now South on Irish all the way home.

The next longer ride – this one is almost 50 miles

The next longer ride is just a stretched out version of the Saturday ride. I just ride to the BlueBell boat-ramp, up to the beach then North on Bray Rd. Now just stay on Bray Rd. until you reach Lake Rd. turn left on Genesee Rd. and ride to the end of the road. If you need water (you might need some) there should be a source of water on the East (back) side of the restroom building at the Lake (Buell lake). Now when I'm done resting I head south on Genesee Rd. Then stay on Genesee until I reach Mt. Morris Rd. Now head East until I reach Irish, then ride South all the way home.

Metamora, Lake Minnawanna Ride.

This ride is pretty close to fifty miles so I do this one before my early longer rides and it usually makes me feel good about my physical shape. These days 100Kis good for me. 100K is cool because it is only about 65 miles which lets me do the ride then do something else after a shower and some fresh clothes.

I start out by heading South on Irish Rd. (near Lippincott Blvd.) I ride all the way to the end of the road. Now I turn left and climb up the hill on Perry road. I follow Perry then back to Hill, a left turn to skirt the water feature before it disappears onto the golf course. I'm sill on Hill rd.. I ride all the way to the end of Hill road at M-15.

You have to be careful here since you have to cross M-15. You're at the top of a hill and the traffic often exceeds the speed limit. The good news is that traffic is rather light on the weekend. You just need to cross M-15 (sometimes called State Rd.), and get over to the right shoulder, ride along the shoulder until you reach Hill Rd.

Turn right onto Hill road and continue East on Hill. After a handful of miles the road changes its name to Pratt road. It then shifts North by a few hundred feet. If you're like me you will continue on Pratt road. all the way to Baldwin road (also known as M-24) .

Keep riding East until encountering Herd rd. It only heads South and it goes up a hill. Follow the road til you se the entrance to the park. Ride the park entrance past the entrance guard shack. The beach is on the left the campers are found on the road that goes right.

At the snack bar near the beach, I often buy a soft pretzel and a Mountain Dew, then I sit back and watch folks enjoy the beach and the lake. If you want to hear some oooo's and aahhh's don't forget to tell the snack bar worker that you just rode from Davison for exercise, double points if you run to the water to cool off first!

To ride home, ride past the park entry hut, be nice, you should wave good-bye to the worker. Ride North back to Pratt road, now ride West till the road name turns back to Hill, then ride to M-15 at the end of Hill Rd. Do you cross the road here or peddle to the South so that you can see the traffic before it climbs the hilll. I tend to cross M-15 where Hill road ends then peddle up the West side of the road then turn on to Perry road and the way home? I ride on Hill then on Perry to the end of Irish Rd. then North home.

chapter 7

Final Thoughts

Your bike or trike will become part of your life, you will be healthier, you will be friendlier, you'll be a better person. I'm not kidding. When you stop with other bikers on any organized ride you will meet new friends who would come to your aid and help you and you would help them. You'll be surprised how good these people are and how friendly they can be,

My glue story

Many years ago I had just finished hooking up several Ethernet switches on a rack. The business owner said why not build me a cover "you know something black that covers the switches and the wires".

I had some Plexiglas and some black paint and a special plastic cutter. I cut the plastic, the top and sides, I glued Velcro to the top of rack

I cut the Plexiglas into four pieces. I needed to glue it together, the top & sides. This would make my cover. the top would hang from the top of the rack using a strip of Velcro, but the sides and the top have to be glued on. I tried hot glue, two kinds of epoxy, something made by GM for hard plastics. Nothing worked.

I didn't know what glue to use. This required the phone and someone with much more knowledge than I have. I dialed the hobble shop. John, (the shop manager) "I'm trying to glue some pieces of Plexiglas together. I tried all the glues that I have, nothing seems to work.)

"Umm...PFM would do it", John said." I have a tube". I bought the tube and used the glue to assemble the black plastic cover. Not only has the cover stayed together. It is still together ten years later. I used the rest of the tube to repair a book case. I left a message for John that I needed another tube. Wait! my friend Joe told me that PFM is really hard to get. I need to switch to Zap Goo. I found that Zap Goo is nearly as good as PFM, it is available at Lowes stores and glues most things to most other things.

I needed three drops of glue on my trike. Two drops to holding the fiberglass flagstaff to the nylon coupler, one drop holds the brass part of the magnet to the steel brake disk. Look, if you only have one tube of glue in your tool box, Zap Goo is a good choice. It glues just about anything to anything else. It drys fast. It's the best bet.

Is the Tadpole Trike Right for Every Rider?

Through I have talked about my new tadpole trike. It is a very good cycle for me and is a great replacement for my upright bike. There are some problems with the trike. Look around your house, if you see mountains, Alps, Rockies, Pyrenees, Smokies the trike is probably not for you. It's heavy. Even the lightweight models are usually over 40 pounds or twice the weight of a good upright bike. Going anywhere in the mountains requires that you peddle your bike uphill. You may not realize that you have to take you. You might want some lighter stuff. My trike is not well suited for steep hills, it's not so good for grass, it's not good for sand. Your dealer will help you find the right brand and model of bike.

Here, roads where I ride are mostly flat with rolling hills the trike makes a lot of sense for me. With the high pressure tires I get around pretty well and I'm able to coast about the same way I do on my upright bike. The trike removes the chance of my lost balance flaring and is more comfortable to ride than my Cannondale, Things I have noticed about the Sun trike is the ball bearing steering tubes, the single walled, machine -made wheels, the direct steering and the mechanical disc brake controls on the handlebars.

t

www.ingramcontent.com/pod-product-compliance
Lightning Source LLC
Chambersburg PA
CBHW030105300526
45785CB00019B/2747